SELF AWARENESS

Copyright © 2019 by Meredith Lynch

All rights reserved. No part of this book may be reproduced or used in any manner without written permission of the copyright owner.

First paperback edition November 2019

ISBN 978-1-7031-5850-2 (paperback)

www.mereandco.com

DISCLAIMER:
This journal is for information purposes only. This is not medical, mental health, financial, religious, or legal advice. Although the Author has made every effort to ensure that the information in this book was correct at press time, the Author will not be held liable in any part for any loss, damage, or disruption caused by this book. The author and/or distributors are not responsible for any adverse effects resulting from this use of the suggestions outlined in this journal. This journal makes no claims or guarantees: your success depends primarily on your own effort, motivation, commitment and follow-through.

HOW TO USE THIS JOURNAL

This journal is a tool to help you become more aware of yourself. It's intended to help you be honest with yourself so that you can grow in whatever way that is meaningful for you right now.

The journal covers 30 days. Each section will help you draw connections between your mind, body, and spirit. Keep close to your bed with a pen so you can complete it first thing when you wake and once you get into bed. You will not need to complete all 30 days to become more self-aware. Revisit this tool throughout your journey, it will always help you grow.

Pay attention to what comes easily and what you find that you're avoiding. Notice patterns you repeat and how you feel. Make connections between what you notice in a good mood and what you notice when you're in a not so great mood. Once you are able to see what you are *ready* to see, you will be able to determine what behaviors are worth keeping or worth adjusting in some way.

Trust that your consciousness is communicating with you and everything you are uncovering is happening at exactly the right time.

Morning

Record the date and the time(s) you woke up.

Dreams

Right when you wake up, while it's freshest in your mind, record as much of your dream(s) as possible. You can be as detailed as you feel. Sometimes it might be specific, at other times you might just remember pieces, feelings, symbols, or people. Write what you can. You may notice this to be a difficult task at first, especially if you don't often remember your dreams. By taking a few seconds each morning to focus your energy on your dreams, you are signalling to your subconscious mind that you're open to using this method of communication. You will find with repeated attention, memories of your dreams will come easier. Most often our dreams contain pieces of our waking life that stick with us (something you watched on tv recently, a stressor on your mind, etc.), but they can also include messages from your subconscious. See if you start to notice any patterns here. You may start to see how food, stress, mood, etc. can impact the dreams you have/remember. There are plenty of excellent dream dictionary resources online that can help you decode subconscious meanings.

Body

Use this space to record anything you are noticing about your physical body in the morning. Everything from muscle pains, bruises, pimples, headaches, if you had restful sleep, etc. Anything you notice is what you're meant to focus on. You may start by focusing on the outside of the body (skin, nails, etc) before moving deeper inward (muscles, tension, spasms, etc). What are you noticing? What is repeating? As you look to analyze how your body is communicating with you, you might consider researching different energy points. You can easily find infographics for the chakras, emotional pain body, reflexology foot and hand maps, acupressure points, and more.

Gratitude

Take this space to develop a gratitude practice. Whatever comes to mind in the moment. You can say the same thing every day. You can be thankful for yourself. You can be grateful for the cup of coffee you're longing for. This is for you. There are no judgements. When you begin to physically write out what you're grateful for, you'll find more and more things to be grateful for. This is a practice to open your heart, your mind, and your abundance.

Intention

In a perfect world, we should strive to do everything with intention. Our subconscious minds crave direction; by consciously stating an intention for the day, we are essentially delivering those orders to our body. Some days you might intend to accomplish specific goals, while on other days you might just intend to be kind. Don't overthink it. Write whatever you instinctively feel. You can have multiple intentions, and you can change your intention(s) every day.

Affirmations

An affirmation practice is a great way to speak things into existence. Words have power. Focused use will shift your mindset to help you control emotions, find peace, manifest money -- there is really no limit here. You can repeat the same affirmations everyday or create new ones. Try to make at least one affirmation relate to your intention (to help achieve that for the day). Affirmations don't all need to be "I AM..." statements. Make sure all statements are written in the present tense (as though they are already achieved) and avoid using any negative language (like "not" or "no"). For example: "I am debt free" is better than "I have no debt".

Morning Ritual

This is to help you remember parts of your morning ritual/routine that you want to hold yourself accountable for. Perhaps you want to be more consistent with your meditation practice, vitamin regimen, or anti-wrinkle routine. Give yourself sometime before you start this journal to see what would work for you here. Keep it limited-- don't overwhelm yourself. The goal is to check the boxes. You can change this as often as you like. If you are trying to develop a ritual, write these bullet points in for several days ahead so you don't forget.

Daily Goals

Pick 3 things you can easily accomplish that day. This could be as simple as daily errands or as big as tasks you've been putting off. It can be helpful to fill out daily goals the night before, especially if you remind yourself of something you need to do before you go to sleep.

Feels

This is a section for you to write whatever you feel. It could be expanding on your dream or body sections, a stream of consciousness writing of what's in your head, follow a prompt, whatever. Some days you might fill every inch of the space, while on other days you will only write two lines --this is for you, there are no rules.

Evening

Record the date and the time you got into bed. If you're tracking your sleeping habits, note the time you actually fall asleep the next morning.

Evening Ritual

Just like in the morning, create an evening ritual/routine for yourself. This could include things like: meditation, a soothing tea, reading a book, or flossing. Give some thought here. Keep it limited and don't overwhelm yourself. Fill in this section for several days in advance so you don't have to think about it every night.

Daily Spending

Just as it sounds-- list out what money you've spent that day. This isn't for tax purposes, so you don't need to be precise. Keep track of what the purchase was for (like clothes, wine, movie tickets). Feel free to mark if it was cash or credit. You are just recording to notice patterns. This section can often be one of the most avoided; however, if you are trying to increase your abundance, it is one of the most helpful.

Intake

This section is to track what you're putting into your body. It is not recommended to specifically record calories-- get an app for that. Just what you're eating & maybe when (especially if you're suffering from poor energy levels). You will start to make connections between your intake and your body, mood & sleep. **If you feel triggered by this section in any way, DO NOT USE IT.** Get creative and see what you feel would be a better fit to track here or just skip it.

Water - Track your water intake for the day. Recommended daily water intake should be half your body weight in fluid ounces (i.e., 120lbs= 60 fl oz of water)

Television - Track how many hours of television you watched that day. If you do not watch television, you can substitute any other vice or habit you'd like to track here.

Custom - These spaces are intentionally left blank for you to fill in with your own habits or vices to track. What do you want to be more aware of? Coffee, nicotine, alcohol, time spent on social media? Create easy graphics you can draw each day for these sections.

Activity

Record any of your physical activity for the day. Taking the stairs, going to cross fit, walking the dog -- anything.

Today's Accomplishments

What did you accomplish today? Big or small. Every win counts. Perhaps you completed your daily goals, worked out, didn't spend any money, or kept your cool in a heated situation. You should be able to write at least 3 things everyday. If you're having a hard time with this section then you're being too hard on yourself.

Gratitude

Round out your day with an evening gratitude practice. Much like your morning practice, just let the gratitude flow effortlessly and without judgement.

Intention

Just like in the morning, we give our subconscious the marching orders for our sleep. Try setting the intention to remember your dreams, have a restful night sleep, restore your energy, raise your vibration, or instruct your body to heal itself.

Feels

This section can once again be used for whatever you want. Reflect on the day, on your tomorrow, on whatever is weighing on your mind. Try a stream of consciousness practice where you just write, non-stop, without worrying about if what you're writing makes sense. You're the only one who will read this, so don't overthink it. This "data dump" from your brain allows you to get all of these thoughts out of your mind so you can rest easier.

ONLY
YOU CAN
CHANGE
YOUR
LIFE.

DATE: /   /

DREAMS

BODY

GRATITUDE

INTENTION

AFFIRMATIONS

MORNING RITUAL
- [ ]
- [ ]
- [ ]
- [ ]
- [ ]

TODAY'S GOALS
- [ ]
- [ ]
- [ ]
- [ ]
- [ ]

FEELS

DATE: ___ / ___ / _____   _____

EVENING RITUAL

- [ ] _____
- [ ] _____
- [ ] _____
- [ ] _____
- [ ] _____

DAILY SPENDING

_____
_____
_____
_____
_____

INTAKE _____
_____
_____

🥛 = _____   🖥 = _____   = _____   = _____

ACTIVITY _____

TODAY'S ACCOMPLISHMENTS
_____
_____
_____

GRATITUDE _____
_____
_____
_____
_____

INTENTION _____
_____
_____
_____
_____

FEELS

☼ DATE: /   /   _____

DREAMS _____

_____
_____
_____
_____
_____
_____
_____
_____
_____

BODY _____

_____
_____
_____
_____
_____
_____

GRATITUDE _____

_____
_____
_____
_____
_____

INTENTION _____

_____
_____
_____
_____

AFFIRMATIONS

MORNING RITUAL

- [ ]
- [ ]
- [ ]
- [ ]
- [ ]

TODAY'S GOALS

- [ ]
- [ ]
- [ ]
- [ ]
- [ ]

FEELS

☾ DATE: ___ / ___ / ___ _____

EVENING RITUAL   DAILY SPENDING

☐ _____   _____
☐ _____   _____
☐ _____   _____
☐ _____   _____
☐ _____   _____

INTAKE _____
_____
_____

🥛 = _____   🖥 = _____   = _____   = _____

ACTIVITY _____

TODAY'S ACCOMPLISHMENTS
_____
_____
_____

GRATITUDE _____
_____
_____
_____
_____

INTENTION _____
_____
_____
_____
_____

FEELS

☼ DATE: /   /   _____

DREAMS _____

BODY _____

GRATITUDE _____

INTENTION _____

AFFIRMATIONS

MORNING RITUAL	TODAY'S GOALS
☐	☐
☐	☐
☐	☐
☐	☐
☐	☐

FEELS

DATE: ___ / ___ / _____

EVENING RITUAL

- ☐ _____
- ☐ _____
- ☐ _____
- ☐ _____
- ☐ _____

DAILY SPENDING

_____
_____
_____
_____
_____

INTAKE _____

🥛 = _____   🖥 = _____   = _____   = _____

ACTIVITY _____

TODAY'S ACCOMPLISHMENTS

_____
_____
_____

GRATITUDE _____

_____
_____
_____
_____

INTENTION _____

_____
_____
_____
_____

FEELS

DATE: / /

DREAMS

BODY

GRATITUDE

INTENTION

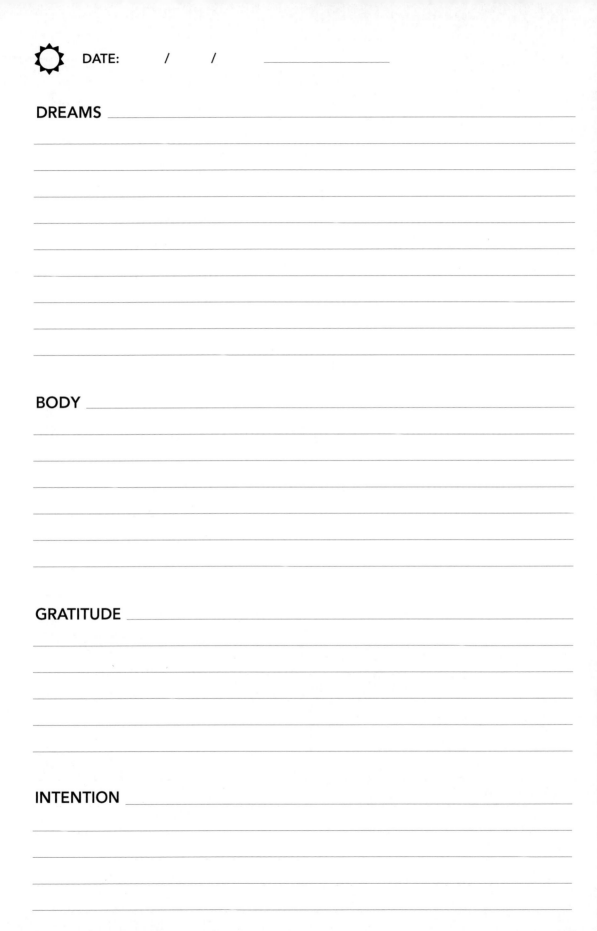

AFFIRMATIONS

MORNING RITUAL

- [ ]
- [ ]
- [ ]
- [ ]
- [ ]

TODAY'S GOALS

- [ ]
- [ ]
- [ ]
- [ ]
- [ ]

FEELS

☾ DATE: ___ / ___ / ___ _____

EVENING RITUAL

☐ _____
☐ _____
☐ _____
☐ _____
☐ _____

DAILY SPENDING

_____
_____
_____
_____
_____

INTAKE _____
_____
_____

🥤 = ___   🖥 = ___   = ___   = ___

ACTIVITY _____

TODAY'S ACCOMPLISHMENTS
_____
_____
_____

GRATITUDE _____
_____
_____
_____
_____

INTENTION _____
_____
_____
_____
_____

FEELS

☼ DATE: /   /   _____

DREAMS _____

BODY _____

GRATITUDE _____

INTENTION _____

AFFIRMATIONS

MORNING RITUAL

- [ ]
- [ ]
- [ ]
- [ ]
- [ ]

TODAY'S GOALS

- [ ]
- [ ]
- [ ]
- [ ]
- [ ]

FEELS

☾ DATE: ___ / ___ / ___ _____

EVENING RITUAL   DAILY SPENDING

☐ _____   _____
☐ _____   _____
☐ _____   _____
☐ _____   _____
☐ _____   _____

INTAKE _____
_____
_____

🥛 = ____   🖥 = ____   = ____   = ____

ACTIVITY _____

TODAY'S ACCOMPLISHMENTS
_____
_____
_____

GRATITUDE _____
_____
_____
_____
_____

INTENTION _____
_____
_____
_____
_____

FEELS

DATE: /   /

DREAMS

BODY

GRATITUDE

INTENTION

AFFIRMATIONS

MORNING RITUAL

- [ ]
- [ ]
- [ ]
- [ ]
- [ ]

TODAY'S GOALS

- [ ]
- [ ]
- [ ]
- [ ]
- [ ]

FEELS

DATE: /   /   _____

EVENING RITUAL

- [ ] _____
- [ ] _____
- [ ] _____
- [ ] _____
- [ ] _____

DAILY SPENDING

_____
_____
_____
_____
_____

INTAKE
_____
_____
_____

🥛 =   🖥 =   =   =

ACTIVITY
_____

TODAY'S ACCOMPLISHMENTS
_____
_____
_____

GRATITUDE
_____
_____
_____
_____
_____

INTENTION
_____
_____
_____
_____

FEELS

☼ DATE: / /

DREAMS

BODY

GRATITUDE

INTENTION

AFFIRMATIONS

MORNING RITUAL

- [ ]
- [ ]
- [ ]
- [ ]
- [ ]

TODAY'S GOALS

- [ ]
- [ ]
- [ ]
- [ ]
- [ ]

FEELS

☾ DATE: ___ / ___ / ___ _____

EVENING RITUAL   DAILY SPENDING

☐ _____   _____
☐ _____   _____
☐ _____   _____
☐ _____   _____
☐ _____   _____

INTAKE _____
_____
_____

🥛 = _____   🖥 = _____   = _____   = _____

ACTIVITY _____

TODAY'S ACCOMPLISHMENTS
_____
_____
_____

GRATITUDE _____
_____
_____
_____
_____

INTENTION _____
_____
_____
_____
_____

FEELS

☼ DATE: /   /   _____

DREAMS _____

BODY _____

GRATITUDE _____

INTENTION _____

AFFIRMATIONS

MORNING RITUAL

- [ ]
- [ ]
- [ ]
- [ ]
- [ ]

TODAY'S GOALS

- [ ]
- [ ]
- [ ]
- [ ]
- [ ]

FEELS

DATE: ___ / ___ / ___   _____

EVENING RITUAL

- [ ] _____
- [ ] _____
- [ ] _____
- [ ] _____
- [ ] _____

DAILY SPENDING

_____
_____
_____
_____
_____

INTAKE _____

🥛 = _____   🖥 = _____   = _____   = _____

ACTIVITY _____

TODAY'S ACCOMPLISHMENTS

_____
_____
_____

GRATITUDE _____

_____
_____
_____
_____

INTENTION _____

_____
_____
_____
_____

FEELS

DATE: /   /

DREAMS

BODY

GRATITUDE

INTENTION

AFFIRMATIONS

MORNING RITUAL	TODAY'S GOALS
☐	☐
☐	☐
☐	☐
☐	☐
☐	☐

FEELS

DATE: / / _____

EVENING RITUAL

DAILY SPENDING

- [ ] _____
- [ ] _____
- [ ] _____
- [ ] _____
- [ ] _____

INTAKE _____

🥛 =   🖥 =   =   =

ACTIVITY _____

TODAY'S ACCOMPLISHMENTS

GRATITUDE

INTENTION

FEELS

☼ DATE: /   /   _____

DREAMS _____

BODY _____

GRATITUDE _____

INTENTION _____

AFFIRMATIONS

MORNING RITUAL

- [ ]
- [ ]
- [ ]
- [ ]
- [ ]

TODAY'S GOALS

- [ ]
- [ ]
- [ ]
- [ ]
- [ ]

FEELS

🌙 DATE: ___ / ___ / ___   _____

EVENING RITUAL

- [ ] _____
- [ ] _____
- [ ] _____
- [ ] _____
- [ ] _____

DAILY SPENDING

_____
_____
_____
_____
_____

INTAKE

_____
_____
_____

🥛 =   🖥 =   =   =

ACTIVITY _____

TODAY'S ACCOMPLISHMENTS

_____
_____
_____

GRATITUDE

_____
_____
_____
_____

INTENTION

_____
_____
_____
_____

FEELS

☼ DATE: / / _____

DREAMS _____

BODY _____

GRATITUDE _____

INTENTION _____

AFFIRMATIONS

MORNING RITUAL

- [ ]
- [ ]
- [ ]
- [ ]
- [ ]

TODAY'S GOALS

- [ ]
- [ ]
- [ ]
- [ ]
- [ ]

FEELS

DATE: / / _____

EVENING RITUAL

☐ _____
☐ _____
☐ _____
☐ _____
☐ _____

DAILY SPENDING

_____
_____
_____
_____
_____

INTAKE _____

🥛 =   🖥 =   =   =

ACTIVITY _____

TODAY'S ACCOMPLISHMENTS

GRATITUDE

INTENTION

FEELS

☼ DATE: /   /   _____

DREAMS _____

_____
_____
_____
_____
_____
_____
_____
_____
_____
_____

BODY _____

_____
_____
_____
_____
_____
_____

GRATITUDE _____

_____
_____
_____
_____
_____
_____

INTENTION _____

_____
_____
_____
_____
_____

AFIRMATIONS

MORNING RITUAL

- [ ]
- [ ]
- [ ]
- [ ]
- [ ]

TODAY'S GOALS

- [ ]
- [ ]
- [ ]
- [ ]
- [ ]

FEELS

DATE: /   /

EVENING RITUAL

☐ _____
☐ _____
☐ _____
☐ _____
☐ _____

DAILY SPENDING

_____
_____
_____
_____
_____

INTAKE _____
_____
_____

🥛 =   🖥 =   =   =

ACTIVITY _____

TODAY'S ACCOMPLISHMENTS
_____
_____
_____

GRATITUDE _____
_____
_____
_____
_____

INTENTION _____
_____
_____
_____
_____

FEELS

☼ DATE: /   /   _____

DREAMS _____

_____
_____
_____
_____
_____
_____
_____
_____
_____

BODY _____

_____
_____
_____
_____
_____
_____

GRATITUDE _____

_____
_____
_____
_____
_____

INTENTION _____

_____
_____
_____
_____

AFFIRMATIONS

MORNING RITUAL

- [ ]
- [ ]
- [ ]
- [ ]
- [ ]

TODAY'S GOALS

- [ ]
- [ ]
- [ ]
- [ ]
- [ ]

FEELS

DATE: /   /

EVENING RITUAL

- [ ]
- [ ]
- [ ]
- [ ]
- [ ]

DAILY SPENDING

INTAKE

🥛 =   🖥 =   =   =

ACTIVITY

TODAY'S ACCOMPLISHMENTS

GRATITUDE

INTENTION

FEELS

☼ DATE: /   /   _____

DREAMS _____

BODY _____

GRATITUDE _____

INTENTION _____

AFFIRMATIONS

MORNING RITUAL

- [ ]
- [ ]
- [ ]
- [ ]
- [ ]

TODAY'S GOALS

- [ ]
- [ ]
- [ ]
- [ ]
- [ ]

FEELS

☾ DATE: ___ / ___ / ___ _____

EVENING RITUAL

- [ ] _____
- [ ] _____
- [ ] _____
- [ ] _____
- [ ] _____

DAILY SPENDING

_____
_____
_____
_____
_____

INTAKE _____

🥛 = _____   🖥 = _____   = _____   = _____

ACTIVITY _____

TODAY'S ACCOMPLISHMENTS

_____
_____
_____

GRATITUDE _____

_____
_____
_____
_____

INTENTION _____

_____
_____
_____
_____

FEELS

DATE: /   /

DREAMS

BODY

GRATITUDE

INTENTION

AFFIRMATIONS

MORNING RITUAL
- [ ]
- [ ]
- [ ]
- [ ]
- [ ]

TODAY'S GOALS
- [ ]
- [ ]
- [ ]
- [ ]
- [ ]

FEELS

🌙 DATE: /   /   _____

EVENING RITUAL

- [ ] _____
- [ ] _____
- [ ] _____
- [ ] _____
- [ ] _____

DAILY SPENDING

_____
_____
_____
_____
_____

INTAKE

_____
_____

🥛 =   🖥 =   =   =

ACTIVITY

_____

TODAY'S ACCOMPLISHMENTS

_____
_____
_____

GRATITUDE

_____
_____
_____
_____
_____

INTENTION

_____
_____
_____
_____

FEELS

☀ DATE: /   /   _____

DREAMS _____

_____
_____
_____
_____
_____
_____
_____
_____
_____
_____

BODY _____

_____
_____
_____
_____
_____
_____
_____

GRATITUDE _____

_____
_____
_____
_____
_____

INTENTION _____

_____
_____
_____
_____

AFFIRMATIONS

MORNING RITUAL

- [ ]
- [ ]
- [ ]
- [ ]
- [ ]

TODAY'S GOALS

- [ ]
- [ ]
- [ ]
- [ ]
- [ ]

FEELS

DATE: /   /   _____

EVENING RITUAL   DAILY SPENDING

☐ _____   _____
☐ _____   _____
☐ _____   _____
☐ _____   _____
☐ _____

INTAKE _____
_____
_____

🥛 = _____   🖥 = _____   = _____   = _____

ACTIVITY _____

TODAY'S ACCOMPLISHMENTS
_____
_____
_____

GRATITUDE _____
_____
_____
_____
_____

INTENTION _____
_____
_____
_____
_____

FEELS

DATE: /   /

DREAMS

BODY

GRATITUDE

INTENTION

AFFIRMATIONS

_____
_____
_____
_____
_____
_____

MORNING RITUAL

- [ ]
- [ ]
- [ ]
- [ ]
- [ ]

TODAY'S GOALS

- [ ]
- [ ]
- [ ]
- [ ]
- [ ]

FEELS

_____
_____
_____
_____
_____
_____
_____
_____
_____
_____
_____
_____
_____
_____
_____
_____
_____
_____

DATE: / / _____

EVENING RITUAL

- [ ] _____
- [ ] _____
- [ ] _____
- [ ] _____
- [ ] _____

DAILY SPENDING

_____
_____
_____
_____
_____

INTAKE _____

🥛 =   🖥 =   =   =

ACTIVITY _____

TODAY'S ACCOMPLISHMENTS

_____
_____
_____

GRATITUDE _____

_____
_____
_____
_____

INTENTION _____

_____
_____
_____
_____

FEELS

☼ DATE: /   /   _____

DREAMS _____

BODY _____

GRATITUDE _____

INTENTION _____

AFFIRMATIONS

MORNING RITUAL	TODAY'S GOALS
☐	☐
☐	☐
☐	☐
☐	☐
☐	☐

FEELS

🌙 DATE: ___ / ___ / ___   _____

EVENING RITUAL   ## DAILY SPENDING

☐ _____   _____
☐ _____   _____
☐ _____   _____
☐ _____   _____
☐ _____

INTAKE _____

🥛 =   🖥 =   =   =

ACTIVITY _____

TODAY'S ACCOMPLISHMENTS

GRATITUDE

INTENTION

FEELS

☼ DATE: /   /   _____

DREAMS _____

_____
_____
_____
_____
_____
_____
_____
_____
_____
_____
_____

BODY _____

_____
_____
_____
_____
_____
_____

GRATITUDE _____

_____
_____
_____
_____
_____
_____

INTENTION _____

_____
_____
_____
_____
_____

AFFIRMATIONS

MORNING RITUAL

- [ ]
- [ ]
- [ ]
- [ ]
- [ ]

TODAY'S GOALS

- [ ]
- [ ]
- [ ]
- [ ]
- [ ]

FEELS

☾ DATE: / / _____

EVENING RITUAL   DAILY SPENDING

☐ _____   _____
☐ _____   _____
☐ _____   _____
☐ _____   _____
☐ _____   _____

INTAKE _____
_____
_____

▯ = _____   ▭ = _____   = _____   = _____

ACTIVITY _____

TODAY'S ACCOMPLISHMENTS
_____
_____
_____

GRATITUDE _____
_____
_____
_____
_____

INTENTION _____
_____
_____
_____
_____

FEELS

☼ DATE: /   /   _____

DREAMS _____

_____
_____
_____
_____
_____
_____
_____
_____
_____
_____
_____

BODY _____

_____
_____
_____
_____
_____
_____
_____

GRATITUDE _____

_____
_____
_____
_____
_____
_____

INTENTION _____

_____
_____
_____
_____

AFFIRMATIONS

MORNING RITUAL

- [ ]
- [ ]
- [ ]
- [ ]
- [ ]

TODAY'S GOALS

- [ ]
- [ ]
- [ ]
- [ ]
- [ ]

FEELS

DATE: /   /   _____

EVENING RITUAL

- [ ] _____
- [ ] _____
- [ ] _____
- [ ] _____
- [ ] _____

DAILY SPENDING

_____
_____
_____
_____
_____

INTAKE _____

🥛 =   🖥 =   =   =

ACTIVITY _____

TODAY'S ACCOMPLISHMENTS

_____
_____
_____

GRATITUDE _____

_____
_____
_____
_____

INTENTION _____

_____
_____
_____
_____

FEELS

DATE: / /

DREAMS

BODY

GRATITUDE

INTENTION

AFFIRMATIONS

MORNING RITUAL
- [ ]
- [ ]
- [ ]
- [ ]
- [ ]

TODAY'S GOALS
- [ ]
- [ ]
- [ ]
- [ ]
- [ ]

FEELS

DATE: /   /   _____

EVENING RITUAL

☐ _____
☐ _____
☐ _____
☐ _____
☐ _____

DAILY SPENDING

_____
_____
_____
_____
_____

INTAKE _____

🥛 =   🖥 =   =   =

ACTIVITY _____

TODAY'S ACCOMPLISHMENTS

_____
_____
_____

GRATITUDE _____

_____
_____
_____
_____

INTENTION _____

_____
_____
_____
_____

FEELS

DATE: / /

DREAMS

BODY

GRATITUDE

INTENTION

AFFIRMATIONS

MORNING RITUAL

- [ ]
- [ ]
- [ ]
- [ ]
- [ ]

TODAY'S GOALS

- [ ]
- [ ]
- [ ]
- [ ]
- [ ]

FEELS

DATE: /   /

EVENING RITUAL

DAILY SPENDING

- [ ]
- [ ]
- [ ]
- [ ]
- [ ]

INTAKE

☐ =   💻 =   =   =

ACTIVITY

TODAY'S ACCOMPLISHMENTS

GRATITUDE

INTENTION

FEELS

DATE: / / _____

DREAMS _____

_____
_____
_____
_____
_____
_____
_____
_____
_____

BODY _____

_____
_____
_____
_____
_____
_____

GRATITUDE _____

_____
_____
_____
_____
_____

INTENTION _____

_____
_____
_____
_____

AFFIRMATIONS

MORNING RITUAL
- [ ]
- [ ]
- [ ]
- [ ]
- [ ]

TODAY'S GOALS
- [ ]
- [ ]
- [ ]
- [ ]
- [ ]

FEELS

☾ DATE: ___ / ___ / ___ _____

EVENING RITUAL

☐ _____
☐ _____
☐ _____
☐ _____
☐ _____

DAILY SPENDING

_____
_____
_____
_____
_____

INTAKE _____
_____
_____

🥛 =   🖥 =   =   =

ACTIVITY _____

TODAY'S ACCOMPLISHMENTS
_____
_____
_____

GRATITUDE _____
_____
_____
_____
_____

INTENTION _____
_____
_____
_____
_____

FEELS

☼ DATE: /   /   _____

DREAMS _____

BODY _____

GRATITUDE _____

INTENTION _____

AFFIRMATIONS

MORNING RITUAL
- [ ]
- [ ]
- [ ]
- [ ]
- [ ]

TODAY'S GOALS
- [ ]
- [ ]
- [ ]
- [ ]
- [ ]

FEELS

DATE: /   /

EVENING RITUAL

- [ ]
- [ ]
- [ ]
- [ ]
- [ ]

DAILY SPENDING

INTAKE

🥛 =   🖥 =   =   =

ACTIVITY

TODAY'S ACCOMPLISHMENTS

GRATITUDE

INTENTION

FEELS

DATE: /   /

DREAMS

BODY

GRATITUDE

INTENTION

AFFIRMATIONS

MORNING RITUAL
- [ ]
- [ ]
- [ ]
- [ ]
- [ ]

TODAY'S GOALS
- [ ]
- [ ]
- [ ]
- [ ]
- [ ]

FEELS

DATE: ___ / ___ / _____

EVENING RITUAL

- [ ] _____
- [ ] _____
- [ ] _____
- [ ] _____
- [ ] _____

DAILY SPENDING

_____
_____
_____
_____
_____

INTAKE

_____

🥛 =   🖥 =   =   =

ACTIVITY

TODAY'S ACCOMPLISHMENTS

GRATITUDE

INTENTION

FEELS

DATE: / /

DREAMS

BODY

GRATITUDE

INTENTION

AFFIRMATIONS

MORNING RITUAL
- [ ]
- [ ]
- [ ]
- [ ]
- [ ]

TODAY'S GOALS
- [ ]
- [ ]
- [ ]
- [ ]
- [ ]

FEELS

☾ DATE: / / _____

EVENING RITUAL

☐ _____
☐ _____
☐ _____
☐ _____
☐ _____

DAILY SPENDING

_____
_____
_____
_____
_____

INTAKE _____

▽ = _____   🖥 = _____   = _____   = _____

ACTIVITY _____

TODAY'S ACCOMPLISHMENTS

_____
_____
_____

GRATITUDE _____

_____
_____
_____
_____

INTENTION _____

_____
_____
_____
_____

FEELS

DATE: /   /

DREAMS

BODY

GRATITUDE

INTENTION

AFFIRMATIONS

MORNING RITUAL	TODAY'S GOALS
☐	☐
☐	☐
☐	☐
☐	☐
☐	☐

FEELS

☾ DATE: / / _____

EVENING RITUAL   ## DAILY SPENDING

☐ _____   _____
☐ _____   _____
☐ _____   _____
☐ _____   _____
☐ _____   _____

INTAKE _____
_____

🥛 = _____   🖥 = _____   = _____   = _____

ACTIVITY _____

TODAY'S ACCOMPLISHMENTS
_____
_____
_____

GRATITUDE _____
_____
_____
_____
_____

INTENTION _____
_____
_____
_____
_____

FEELS

DATE: / /

DREAMS

BODY

GRATITUDE

INTENTION

AFFIRMATIONS

MORNING RITUAL
- [ ]
- [ ]
- [ ]
- [ ]
- [ ]

TODAY'S GOALS
- [ ]
- [ ]
- [ ]
- [ ]
- [ ]

FEELS

☾ DATE: ___ / ___ / ___ _____

EVENING RITUAL   DAILY SPENDING

☐ _____   _____
☐ _____   _____
☐ _____   _____
☐ _____   _____
☐ _____   _____

INTAKE _____
_____
_____

🥛 = _____   🖥 = _____   = _____   = _____

ACTIVITY _____

TODAY'S ACCOMPLISHMENTS
_____
_____
_____

GRATITUDE _____
_____
_____
_____
_____

INTENTION _____
_____
_____
_____
_____

FEELS

DATE: / / _____

DREAMS _____

_____
_____
_____
_____
_____
_____
_____
_____
_____

BODY _____

_____
_____
_____
_____
_____

GRATITUDE _____

_____
_____
_____
_____
_____

INTENTION _____

_____
_____
_____
_____

AFFIRMATIONS

MORNING RITUAL

☐ ___
☐ ___
☐ ___
☐ ___
☐ ___

TODAY'S GOALS

☐ ___
☐ ___
☐ ___
☐ ___
☐ ___

FEELS

DATE: ___ / ___ / _____

EVENING RITUAL

- ☐ _____
- ☐ _____
- ☐ _____
- ☐ _____
- ☐ _____

DAILY SPENDING

_____
_____
_____
_____
_____

INTAKE _____

🥛 = _____   🖥 = _____   = _____   = _____

ACTIVITY _____

TODAY'S ACCOMPLISHMENTS
_____
_____
_____

GRATITUDE _____
_____
_____
_____

INTENTION _____
_____
_____
_____

FEELS

DATE: ___/___/___ _____

DREAMS _____

_____
_____
_____
_____
_____
_____
_____
_____
_____
_____

BODY _____

_____
_____
_____
_____
_____
_____

GRATITUDE _____

_____
_____
_____
_____
_____

INTENTION _____

_____
_____
_____
_____

AFFIRMATIONS

MORNING RITUAL

- [ ]
- [ ]
- [ ]
- [ ]
- [ ]

TODAY'S GOALS

- [ ]
- [ ]
- [ ]
- [ ]
- [ ]

FEELS

DATE: /   /   _____

EVENING RITUAL

- [ ] _____
- [ ] _____
- [ ] _____
- [ ] _____
- [ ] _____

DAILY SPENDING

_____
_____
_____
_____
_____

INTAKE _____

_____

_____

🥛 =   🖥 =   =   =

ACTIVITY _____

TODAY'S ACCOMPLISHMENTS

_____
_____
_____

GRATITUDE _____

_____
_____
_____
_____

INTENTION _____

_____
_____
_____
_____

FEELS

Manufactured by Amazon.ca
Bolton, ON